SRA Reading Mastery Plus

Workbook B

Level 2

SRA
A Division of The McGraw-Hill Companies

Columbus, Ohio

www.sra4kids.com

SRA/McGraw-Hill

*A Division of The **McGraw·Hill** Companies*

Copyright © 2002 by SRA/McGraw-Hill.

All rights reserved. Except as permitted under the United States
Copyright Act, no part of this publication may be reproduced or
distributed in any form or by any means, or stored in a database
or retrieval system, without the prior written permission of the
publisher, unless otherwise indicated.

Send all inquiries to:
SRA/McGraw-Hill
8787 Orion Place
Columbus, OH 43240-4027

Printed in the United States of America.

ISBN 0-07-569090-X

6 7 8 9 DBH 06 05

Name _____

A.

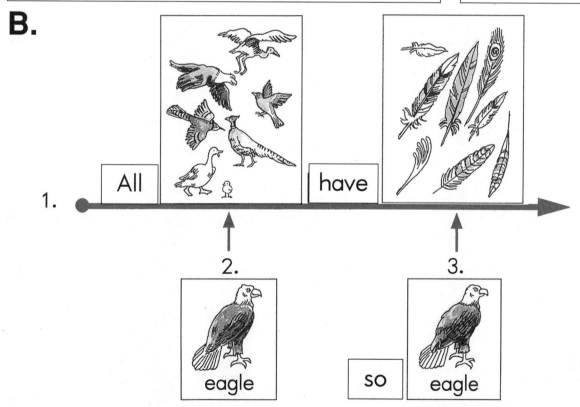

ate a burger

sat under a tree

drove a van

went fishing

ate watermelon

sat on a table

ate pie

B.

1. All [birds] have [feathers]

2. eagle

3. so eagle

ostrich   ostrich

Name _____

C.

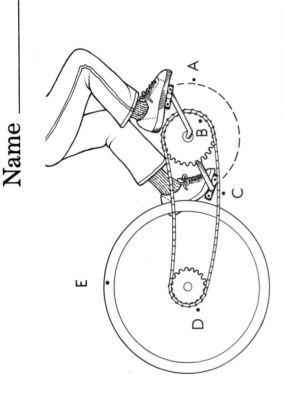

D.

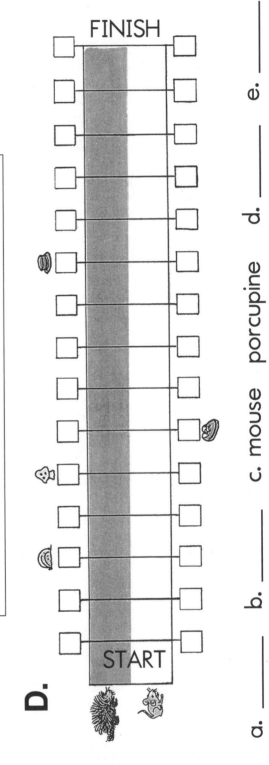

FINISH

START

The porcupine runs 5 feet each second.
The mouse runs 3 feet each second.

a. _____   b. _____   c. mouse   porcupine   d. _____   e. _____

1. Boo had turned the mean ghosts into _____ ghosts.
   sitting   smiling   mean

2. Boo said, "Hog, sog, bumpy _____."

3. Who said, "You must come to live with me"? _____

4. Who was shy? _____

5. Did Boo go to live with the king? _____

6. People went out at night to find _____.
   monsters   farmers   ghosts

★★★

1. Where were Spot and
   the tall girl going? _____

2. Did Spot hear well? _____

3. What did the pig want? _____

The girl sat in her tent.

1. Make a box around the words that tell who sat in the tent.

2. Circle the words that tell where the girl sat.

3. Make an r over the word sat.

The con fox said, "It is getting cold out. I need a new coat. So I will go out and con somebody out of a coat." So the con fox went out. He saw some white coats near a farm house. But when he tried to grab those coats, he found out that they were ghosts. So the con fox ran back to his cold house.

1. Who said, "It is getting cold out"? _____

2. What did the con fox want? _____
      a coat   a box   a sheet

3. So he went to a farm _____.

4. What were the coats? _____
      men   farmers   ghosts

If a girl is swimming, she is tall.

Circle every girl who is tall.

Side 2

Name _____

1. Who was going to genie school? _____

2. Could Ott do a lot of genie tricks? _____

3. Was Ott the best of those in genie school? _____

4. What did Ott make when the teacher told him to make an apple?

_____

      an alligator   an apple   a ship   a genie

5. What did Ott make when the teacher told him to make gold?

a pot of b_____

6. Who ran into the school? _____
      a child   a teacher   an old woman   a yellow bottle

7. Who would have to go to the yellow bottle?

one of the _____
      old genies   teachers   children from school

★★

1. What did the monster turn the king into? _____

2. The monster had a rod made of _____.

3. The monster made Boo part _____ and part ghost.

_____

Three mean ghosts went to the farm.

1. Circle the words that tell who went to the farm.
2. Make a box around the word <u>went</u>.
3. Make a line over the words that tell where the ghosts went.

An elephant lived with jumping bugs. That elephant never saw another elephant. All he saw was bugs. So the elephant tried to be a bug. He tried to jump like a bug. But every time he jumped he made a hole in the ground. The bugs were getting mad at him. They kept saying, "You are not a bug. Stop trying to jump around."

One day the elephant met five other elephants. Now the elephant doesn't jump like a jumping bug. He walks like the other elephants.

1. Who did the elephant live with? _____

2. What did the elephant make when he jumped?

   _____ in the ground

3. Who said, "Stop trying to jump around"? _____

4. Does the elephant jump like a jumping bug now? _____

If a hat is spotted, it is old.

Circle every hat that is old.

Side 2

Name _____

1. What is the name of the genie in this story? _____

2. Who said, "No, no. These children cannot go to work as genies"?

   _____

3. Who said, "I will give the children a test"? _____

4. The old woman said, "Make a _____ appear on the floor."

5. Did Ott make a peach or a beach? a _____

6. Which genie was sent to the yellow bottle? _____

7. What is the title of this story?

   _____

1. How many ghosts lived with Boo? _____

2. Could any of those ghosts read? _____

3. Which ghost could read the words on the magic rod? _____

> The con fox ran fast.

1. Make a box around the word <u>ran</u>.

2. Circle the word that tells how he ran.

3. Make a line under the words that tell who ran fast.

One day Boo was walking down the street. Boo had his magic rod. The monster jumped out and tried to take the rod from Boo. Boo held onto the rod and said, "Bid bide, sap sape."

And what do you think happened to the monster? She turned into a teacher. She smiled. She was nice. She was smart. She was one of the best teachers you have ever seen.

1. What was Boo holding? the magic _____

2. Who wanted to take the rod from Boo? _____

3. Who said magic words? _____

4. What did the monster turn into? _____

If a dog eats grass, she is sick.

Circle every dog that is sick.

Name _____

1. What is the name of the genie in this story? _____

2. Was that genie very good at genie tricks? _____

3. What was the name of the girl
   who found the yellow bottle? _____

4. What street was she on? _____

5. How many boys began to follow Carla? _____

6. Did the boys think there was a genie in the bottle? _____

7. Did Carla really think there was a genie in the bottle? _____

8. Who came out of the bottle when Carla rubbed it? _____

★★★

1. Did Sid send out pine trees or pin trees? _____

2. What did the boss keep in her cane can? _____

3. What did Sid make for the window? _____

Pam tossed the ball over the hill.

1. Make a box around the word <u>tossed</u>.

2. Circle the word that tells who tossed the ball.

3. Make a line under the words that tell where she tossed the ball.

Once there was a bit of ice in an icebox. "It is cold in this icebox," the bit of ice said. "I will go where it is hot."

"If you go where it is hot you will melt," the other bits of ice said. But the bit of ice went to where it was hot. It wasn't long before she saw that she was getting smaller.

"I'm melting," the bit of ice said. "I must go back in the icebox." And she did. Now she is smaller but happy.

1. This story is about a bit of _____ .

2. The ice lived in an ice _____ .

3. Where did the ice want to go? where it is _____

4. What happened to the ice? She began to _____ .

5. Where is the bit of ice now? in the _____

If a tree is bent, it is old.

Circle every tree that is old.

Side 2

1. Who said, "Oh, master Carla, what can I do for you?" _____

2. Who said, "Give those boys a spanking"? _____

3. Did Ott give the boys a spanking or a banking? a _____

4. Ott told Carla that he was a very _____ genie.

5. Was that a lie? _____

6. Did Ott send Carla back home or to Rome? _____

7. What is the title of this story?

_____

★★★

1. What did the tiger have in his pouch? _____
   cash   stones   rocks   tigers

2. What did he get from the man at the stand?

_____

3. He made the cone into a _____ .

The genie looked small.

1. Make a <u>w</u> over the word <u>looked</u>.

2. Circle the word that tells how the genie looked.

3. Make a line under the words that tell what looked small.

A mean man had a bottle with a genie in it. Every day the mean man made the genie do tricks. But the mean man never liked the tricks. One day the mean man said, "I am tired of seeing you make gold appear. Let's see your best trick."

"Yes, master," the genie said. "I will show you my very best trick."

The genie waved his hands and turned the mean man into a log.

1. Who had the bottle? _____

2. Did the mean man like the genie's tricks? _____

3. Who said, "I will show you my very best trick"? _____

4. What did the man turn into? _____

If a man is tired, he is sitting.

Circle every man who is tired.

Name _____

A.

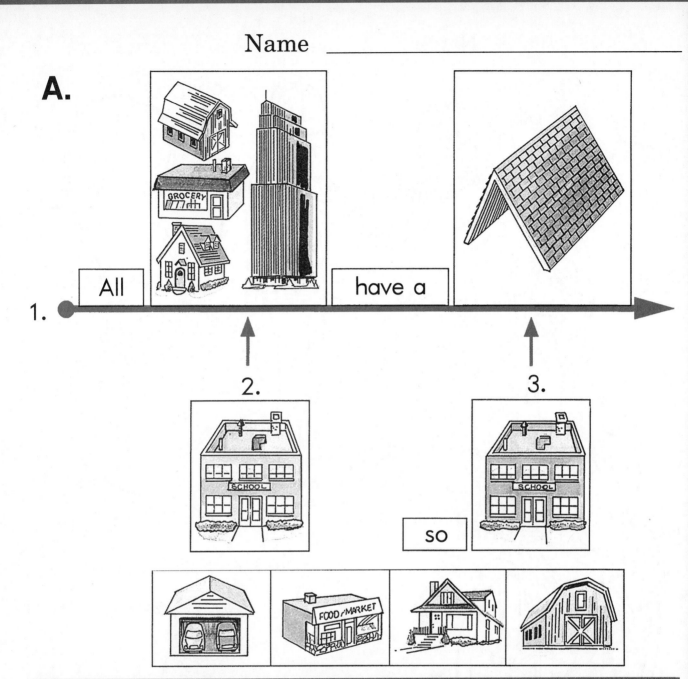

1. ● ——— | All | | have a |

2. | SO |

B. The wise old rat runs 10 feet each second.
The toy car goes 2 feet each second.

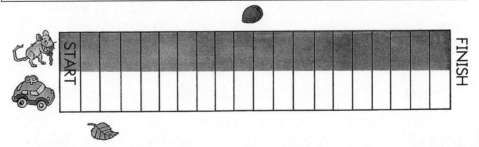

a. _____   b. _____   c. wise old rat   toy car   d. _____

Name _____

C.

Molly

Goober

Mrs. Hudson

Zelda

rode	ate	played	jumped	read	rope
banana		book	violin		bike

1. What is the title of this story?

   _____

2. Where did Ott send Carla from the bank? to _____
        a spanking   her home   Rome   genie school

3. Where did they go from Rome? to _____
        Carla's home   a forest   a lake   a bank

4. Did Ott make an alligator or an apple? an _____

5. Did Ott make a peach or a beach? a _____

6. Who said, "You are a mess of a genie"? _____

7. Did Ott make a hot log or a hot dog? a _____

8. Was Ott happy or sad? _____

★★

1. What did the ghosts
   get from the monster? _____

2. Did they scare the monster? _____

3. Who turned the mean ghosts into happy ghosts? _____

That pile of gold feels cold.

1. Make a box around the words that tell what feels cold.
2. Make a p over the word <u>feels</u>.
3. Circle the word that tells how the pile of gold feels.

One day Spot met Boo the ghost. Boo had a magic rod. Spot said, "I want some bones. What do I say to make bones appear?"

Boo told Spot to hold the rod and say, "Hope, bone, bone, hope."

Spot tried to say that. But what she said was, "Home, cone, cone, home." When Spot said those words, she saw that she could fly like a bird. Now she has fun flying.

1. Who did Spot meet? _____

2. What did Boo have? a magic _____

3. What did Spot want? _____

4. Spot said, "Home, cone, _____, _____."

5. Did Spot make bones appear? _____

Every fat bird likes bugs.

Circle every bird that likes bugs.

Name _____

1. Ott said, "I will make a sound that is very _____."

2. Did Ott make a sound that was loud? _____

3. What did he make? a _____

4. When Ott tried to make a cloud, he made a _____ sound.

5. Who gave Ott a kiss? _____

6. When Ott wished them to go
   to Rome, where did they go? _____

7. Who said, "I don't know how I do that"? _____

8. What is the title of this story?

   _____

1. Dan was a _____.

2. What was the name of the dog that helped the teacher? _____

3. Could that dog read well? _____

4. Did the boys and girls come to class early or late? _____

This elephant sounds loud.

---

1. Circle the word that tells how the elephant sounds.

2. Make a line under the word sounds.

3. Make a box around the words that tell what sounds loud.

There was an alligator that liked to eat
things. She ate a tiger. She ate a monster. She
ate anything that got in her way. Ten bugs got
in her way. She ate them. They tickled inside the
alligator. When the alligator opened her mouth
to laugh, all the animals came out. The tiger,
the monster, and the ten bugs all came out.
Now everybody is happy but the alligator.

1. What did the alligator like to do? _____

2. Who tickled her? _____

3. Did the bugs come out? _____

4. Did the monster come out? _____

5. Is the alligator happy now? _____

Every white box is made of wood.

Circle all the wood boxes.

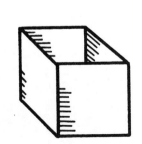

Name _____

1. What was streaming down Carla's cheek? a _____

2. Where were Ott and Carla? in _____

3. Did Ott tell Carla that he had lied to her? _____

4. Who tried to call for help? _____

5. What hit Ott in the face? a _____
     dish   fish   hot dog   beach

6. Who said, "I wish you would get out of here"? _____

7. Where did the bottle go
   when Carla tossed it? _____
        crash   through a window   on the ground   fast

★★★

1. Who began to howl when the
   ghosts got near the castle? _____
        the monster   the hounds   the horse

2. Who was sitting at the table
   when the ghosts floated in? _____
        Boo   the monster   the boss

3. Which ghost could read what it said on the magic rod? _____

_____

A car rolled down the hill.

1. Make a b over the word down.
2. Make a line under the words that tell where the car rolled.
3. Make a line over the words that tell what rolled down the hill.

A girl had six apples. These apples were in her house. The con fox had a plan for getting the apples. He made a big swing near the house. He got on the swing and began to swing very hard. Then he let go and went flying into the girl's house. But he landed in a tub. The girl picked him up and said, "What are you doing in here? You're all wet." So she put him on the line to dry. That con fox is not happy.

1. Who made a swing? _____

2. What was the fox trying to get? _____

3. What did he land in? _____

4. Who hung him on the line? _____

5. Why did she put the fox on the line? _____

All the old coats are Bob's.

Circle every coat that is Bob's.

1. Who went back into the yellow bottle? _____

2. Who came running from the house? _____
       a woman   Ott   a man   Carla

3. The woman said that _____ tossed the
   bottle through the window.
       Ott   an old genie   Carla

4. Who was going to spank Carla? _____

5. Who rubbed the bottle? _____

6. Ott fixed the _____ of glass in the window.
       pan   pane   pine   pin

7. Who said, "Please don't hate me"? _____

★★★

1. Don wanted to be a _____ man.

2. Where did Don work? in a _____ shop

3. When Don turned into a super man, he had a _____

   and a _____ .

The girls were mad.

1. Circle the words that tell who were mad.

2. Make a box around the word <u>were</u>.

3. Make a box around the word that tells how the girls felt.

There was a fat cloud. That cloud was so fat that it could not keep up with the other clouds. The fat cloud became very sad and started to cry. When it cried, big drops of rain fell from the cloud. The cloud got smaller and smaller. Soon the cloud was not fat any more. Now the cloud can keep up with the other clouds.

1. The cloud was _____.

2. Is the cloud fat now? _____

3. Why did the cloud cry? because it could not _____

_____ with the other clouds

4. When the cloud cried, it got s_____.

Every girl can read well.

Circle every child who can read well.

1. What is the title of this story?

   _____

2. Where were Ott and Carla? in _____

3. What did Ott get when he called for help? a _____

        hot dog   pane   peach   fish

4. Carla and Ott went to the park and sat in the _____.

        shad   shade   home   stone

5. Carla found part of the book that said, "How to go _____."

        Rome   bone   home   stone

6. Who began to read the book out loud? _____

★★★

1. Who scared the monster from the castle?

   the mean _____

2. The monster made Boo have a fish tail and a _____.

3. The monster had turned the king into a _____.

> The ball rolled down the hill.

1. Circle the words that tell what rolled down the hill.
2. Make a y over the word <u>rolled</u>.
3. Make a line under the words that tell where the ball rolled.

Jill was a horse with big, big feet. The other horses laughed at Jill. "Ho, ho," they said. "How can you run with those big feet?"

Then it began to rain a lot. The ground became mud. One horse tried to run in the mud but he got stuck. Another horse got stuck. So did another horse. Then Jill ran in the mud. But she did not get stuck. Her feet were too big to get stuck in the mud. The other horses said, "I wish I had big feet." Jill was happy.

1. What did Jill have? _____

2. Did the other horses get stuck in the mud? _____

3. Did Jill get stuck in the mud? _____

4. Who said, "I wish I had big feet"?

_____

Every small window has glass in it.

Circle every window with glass in it.

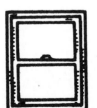
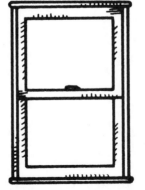
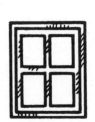

Side 2

A. Name _____

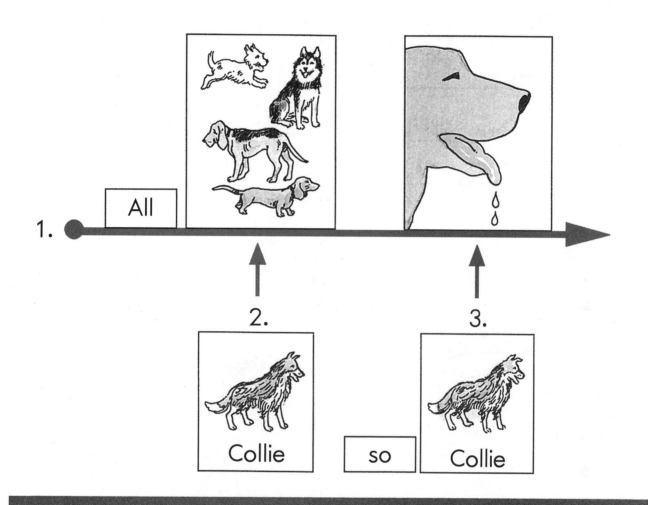

1. ●———[All][dogs] [drooling dog head]——▶

2. ↑ [Collie]

[so] 3. ↑ [Collie]

Poodle | Beagle | puppy | Greyhound

Name _____

C.

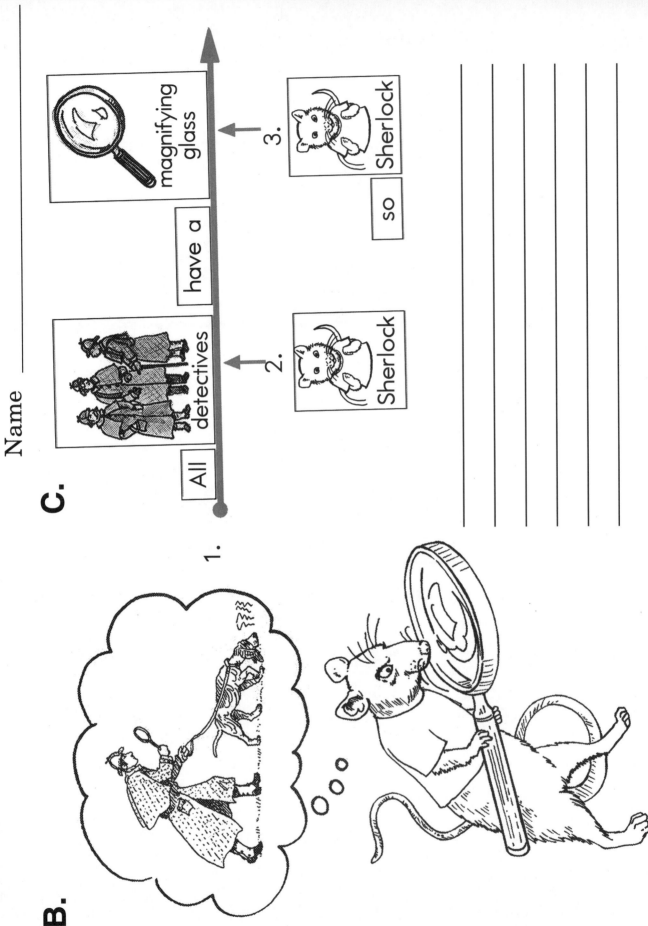

All | detectives | have a | magnifying glass

1.

2. Sherlock

3. so Sherlock

B.

Side 2

Make a line under the answer.

1. Carla was _____ from Ott's school book.
   reading   sitting   laughing

Fill in the blanks.

2. Carla said, "Ib, bub, ib, bub, ib, bub, bibby. Bome, _____,

   _____ . I want to go _____, _____,

   _____ ."

3. Who said, "That is too much to remember"? _____

Circle the answer.

4. Who sent Carla home?
        an old genie   Carla   Ott

Fill in the blanks.

5. Did Ott go to Carla's home? _____

6. Who said, "I better call for help"? _____

★★

Fill in the blanks.

1. Who ran around and made a hole in the school? _____

2. What stopped in front of the school? _____
        a bus   a truck   a tree

3. Who was in the truck? a little _____

4. Who said, "You are too small for this job"? _____

If a cup has spots, it is hot.

Circle every cup that is hot.

There was a king who was very rich. So he had everything made of gold. He had gold tables. He had gold lamps. He even had a gold bed. One day it got very cold out, so he put on his gold hat. Then he put on his gold boots and his gold pants. But he had on so much gold that he could not walk. He is still standing there in his gold things.

Fill in the blanks.

1. The king was very _____.

2. What were his things made of? _____

3. Who put on a gold hat? _____

4. Could the king walk with all those gold things on? _____

Side 2

Name _____

Circle the answer.

1. Carla was reading the part of the book that told how
   to call for _____ .

        home   hounds   horses   help

Fill in the blanks.

2. What is the title of this story?

_____

3. Did a fish drop from the sky when Carla called for help? _____

4. Did the old genie believe that Carla had called for help? _____

5. What did the old genie hold on her head? a _____
           rod   rock   rag   Ron

6. Did Carla turn it into water? _____

Make a line under the answer.

7. Who got mad?
           Ott   the old genie   Carla

Fill in the blanks.

8. Who said, "I need your help"? _____

9. Who did Carla want to find? _____

★★★

Fill in the blanks.

1. How many ghosts lived with Boo? _____

2. Were they nice to Boo? _____

3. Who said, "I have found somebody you can't scare"? _____

If a boy has a hat on, he is cold.

Make a box around every boy who is cold.

Edna was an old lady who could not laugh. Her brother took her to funny shows. But she did not laugh. Then one day, she met a bug. The bug said, "My friends and I can make you laugh."

"No, you can't," Edna said. "Nothing can make me laugh."

So one hundred bugs came over. Ninety bugs sat on the old lady. And ten bugs tickled her and tickled her. She laughed and laughed and laughed.

Circle the answers.

1. What couldn't the old lady do?　　go to shows　　sit　　laugh

2. Who took her to shows?　　her mother　　her brother　　her bugs

Fill in the blanks.

3. Who said, "My friends and I can make you laugh"? _____

4. Who said, "No, you can't"? _____

5. Did the bugs make her laugh? _____

Side 2

Name _____

Fill in the blanks.

1. What is the title
   of this story? _____

2. Did the old genie say that
   humans can't do very simple tricks? _____

Circle the answers.

3. Who said, "I will try to send another genie"?
        the old genie   Carla   Ott

4. Who was she talking to?   Carla   Ott   the teacher

Fill in the blank.

5. Who said, "I don't want another genie"? _____

Make a line over the answers.

6. Which genie did Carla want?
        the old genie   Ott   the teacher

7. Did the old genie let Carla go to genie school?
        Yes   No

If a boy is hungry, he is jumping.

Make a box around every boy who is hungry.

Fill in the blanks.

1. One note from the boss said, "T_____
the oak tree near the door."

2. Another note said, "Send a c_____ to Sam's tree farm."

3. Another note said, "Plant seeds on the s_____."

Viz was a very sad window. He said, "Nobody looks at me. When people are on one side of me, they look at things that are on the other side of me. But they never look at me."

Then one night things got very cold. Ice formed on Viz, the window. The next day everybody said, "Look at the pretty window." Viz was a proud window now.

Fill in the blanks.

1. Who was sad? _____

2. Why was Viz sad? because nobody looked at _____

Make a line over the answer.

3. What happened one night?
Things got cold.   Things got wet.   Things got hot.

Fill in the blanks.

4. What formed on that window? _____

5. Did people look at Viz the next day? _____

Every rat thinks.   Linda is a rat.

What does Linda do? _____

Name _____

Fill in the blanks.

1. What is the title of this story?

   _____

2. When Carla snapped her fingers, a _____ appeared.

3. She told the boy to _____ on the rock.

Make a line over the answers.

4. Then she turned the rock into _____.
       a bottle   water   a genie

5. Who was the best at doing tricks?
       Ott   Carla   a little genie

6. Soon it was time for the children to take their genie _____.
       now   how   vow   cow

If the dog is little, he can run fast.

Make a line under every dog that can run fast.

Fill in the blanks.

1. A tame tiger liked ice c_____.

2. Did the tiger have cash? _____

3. Did the tiger want a con or a cone? _____

A little girl was mad because she was so small. She said, "I wish I was big. I wish I was bigger than anybody."

Boo was hiding near the girl. He took the magic rod and said some magic words. The girl began to grow bigger and bigger. Soon she was as big as a house. Then she began to cry. She said, "I don't like to be so big. I wish I was small again." So Boo made her small again. Now she is happy.

Fill in the blanks.

1. Why was the girl sad? because she was so _____

2. Who said, "I wish I was big"? _____

3. Who made her get bigger and bigger? _____

4. Was the girl happy when she was big? _____

5. She said, "I _____ I was small again."

Every dog pants.   Rob is a dog.

What does Rob do? _____

Side 2

Make a line under the answers.

1. Who told the children about what a genie had to do?
   Ott   Carla   the old genie

2. Who began to cry?
   Ott   Carla   the old genie

3. Was Carla ready to forget about herself
   and do what her master told her?   Yes   No

Fill in the blanks.

4. Was the old genie mad at her? _____

5. Were the other children mad at Carla? _____

6. What is the title of this story?

   _____

7. Did Carla take the genie vow? _____

All of the short boys have dogs.

Make a box around every boy who has a dog.

Fill in the blanks.

1. Spot met a girl who was _____ .

2. The girl and Spot were going to the _____ .

3. The girl got a _____ for Spot.

There was a genie named Itt. He could not do many genie tricks. One day he tried to make a truck appear. But he made a trunk appear. Then he tried to make a hot dog. But he made a hot frog. That frog was mad. He hopped in the pond to cool off.

Fill in the blanks.

1. What was the genie's name? _____

2. What couldn't he do? many genie _____

3. What did he make for a truck? _____

4. What did he make for a hot dog? _____

Every car has doors.   Sid has a car.

What does Sid's car have? _____

Name _____

A.

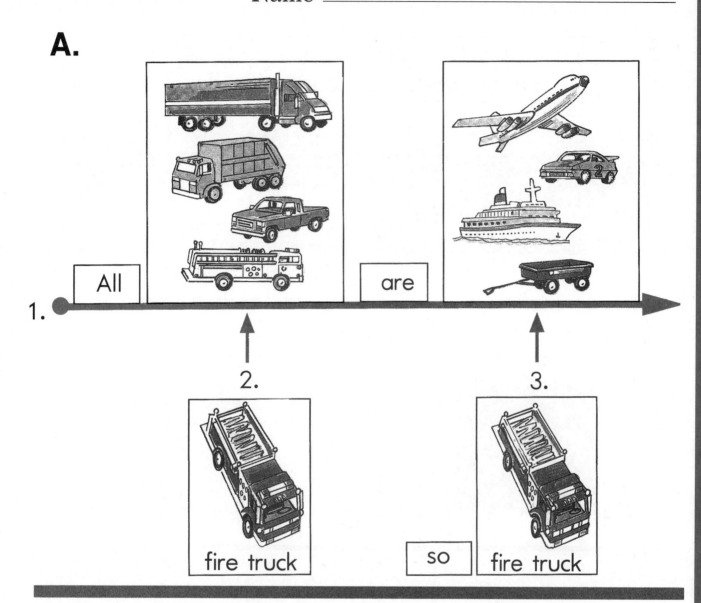

1. All ___ are ___

2. fire truck

3. so fire truck

Name _____

B. | The wise old rat goes 10 feet each second.
The mouse goes 3 feet each second.

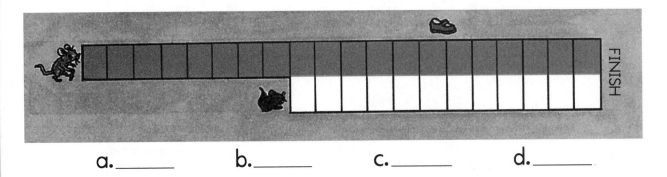

a._____   b._____   c._____   d._____

C.

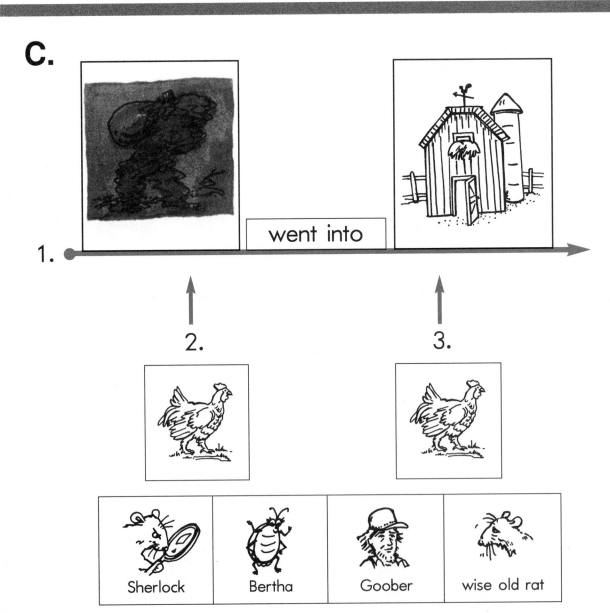

went into

1.

2.   3.

| Sherlock | Bertha | Goober | wise old rat |

Name _____

Fill in the blanks.

1. What is the title
   of this story? _____

2. Which genie went to a yellow
   bottle that belonged to Carla? _____

3. Was Ott happy? _____

Make a box around the answers.

4. Who told the old genie that some new bottles had been found?
   Ott   the teacher   Carla

5. How many bottles were found?   six   five   three

Fill in the blanks.

6. Who is training genies at the school now?

   _____ and _____

7. Is Ott a good teacher? _____

8. Carla is a good teacher because she is very _____.

9. Is there more to come in this story? _____

All the girls with long hair have pets.

Make a line over the girls who have pets.

Fill in the blanks.

1. What did Ott make when he
   tried to make an apple? _____

2. What did Ott make when he
   tried to make a peach? _____

3. Who told Ott that he would have to
   go into the yellow bottle? the old g_____

       Once there was a sad horse. The horse had
flies on his back. He tried to get rid of the
flies but he couldn't. The flies kept biting him
and biting him.
       At last the horse yelled, "I hate flies."
       A bird said, "I don't hate them. I love them."
       The bird hopped on the horse's back and ate
the flies. Now the horse is happy and so is the bird.

Fill in the blank.

1. What did the horse have on his back? _____

Circle the answer.

2. Could the horse get rid of the flies?
        Yes   No

Make a box under the answers.

3. Who said that he loved flies?
        the bird   the farmer   the horse

4. The bird _____ the flies.   kissed   ate   hugged

Every bird eats bugs.   Ron is a bird.

What does Ron do? _____

Name _____

Fill in the blank.

1. Did Kim spell well? _____

Circle the answer.

2. How did Kim spell the word <u>made</u>?   mad   mod   made

Make a box around the answers.

3. How did Kim spell the word <u>van</u>?   von   vane   van

4. How did Kim spell the word <u>mat</u>?   mot   mate   mote

Fill in the blanks.

5. Kim wanted to look under the word _____ in the phone book.

6. But Kim looked under the word _____.

7. The woman said that she would send the vane to Kim's house in _____ minutes.

8. What is the title of this story? _____

All the men with hats have red hair.

Circle the men with red hair.

Fill in the blanks.

1. Did Ott give the mean boys a spanking? _____

2. What did he give them? _____

3. Did Ott send Carla to her home or to Rome? _____

━━━━━━━━━━━━━━━━━━━━━━━━━━━━━━━━━━

There was an old clock that didn't work. The woman who had the clock said, "I will throw this old clock out. It doesn't work." So she did.

A bum looked at the clock and said, "I am a bum. I don't work. That clock doesn't work. So I will get along well with that clock."

Now the bum is happy. He doesn't work and he has a clock that doesn't work.

Make a circle under the answer.

1. Who said, "I will throw this old clock out"?
   the woman   the clock   the bum

Make a box over the answer.

2. Who found the clock?   a woman   a clock   a bum

Fill in the blanks.

3. The bum doesn't _____ and he has a _____

   that doesn't _____ .

━━━━━━━━━━━━━━━━━━━━━━━━━━━━━━━━━━

All children go to school.   Tom and Linda are children.

What do Tom and Linda do? _____

Fill in the blanks.

1. Did Kim need a van or a vane? a _____

2. What did she get? a _____

Make a box around the answer.

3. How did Kim feel?

         mad   made   mate   mat

Circle the answers.

4. Did Kim try to find the word <u>truck</u> or
   the word <u>trunk</u> in the phone book?   truck   trunk

5. Which word did she find?   truck   trunk

Fill in the blanks.

6. Did Kim have to pay for the trunk? _____

7. How many dollars did she have to pay? _____

8. Was Kim very happy? _____

All of the big eggs have chicks in them.

Make a box around every egg with a chick in it.

Fill in the blanks.

1. What did Ott make when he
   tried to make a hot dog? _____

2. What did Ott make when he
   tried to make an apple? _____

3. What did Ott make when he
   tried to make a peach? _____

A snake named Bill was sad because he could not kick the ball. The other animals said, "Ho, Ho. You can't kick a ball. Snakes don't have legs."

Then one day Bill went to the place where the other animals were kicking the ball. Bill said, "I can make the ball go as far as any other animal." He hit the ball with his nose. It went very far.

The other animals said, "That snake doesn't have legs, but he can really kick with his nose."

Circle the answer.

1. The snake was named _____ .   Ball   Bull   Bill

Make a circle under the answer.

2. He could not _____ a ball.   hit   lick   kick

Make a circle over the answer.

3. The other animals said, "Snakes don't have _____ ."

   feet   legs   ears

Every mip is an animal.   Linda has a mip.

What do you know about her mip? _____

Side 2

Name _____

Fill in the blanks.

1. What is the title of this story?

   _____

2. What did Kim get when she
   tried to call for a van? a _____

3. What did Kim get when she
   tried to call for a truck? a _____

Circle the answer.

4. What did Kim look up when she tried to find a rental car?

          dental car   rental care   dental care

Fill in the blanks.

5. What was Kim trying to rent from the man? a _____

6. What did the man think
   Kim was trying to rent? _____

7. Was the man's name under "rental car"? _____

Tim made all the dresses with buttons.

Circle every dress that Tim made.

Side 1

Fill in the blanks.

1. When Ott tried to make a sound that was loud, he made a c_____.

2. When Ott called for help, a _____ hit him in the face.

3. Carla tossed a bottle through a _____.

There was an old bug who could do many tricks. She could drive a car. She could stand on her head. She could sing, but nobody could hear her. She was so small that nobody saw her tricks.

Then one day, she drove a car into a big tent. The girl inside the tent grabbed the bug and said, "This old bug can drive cars. I will put her into my show." And she did. Now the old bug is the star of a show.

Circle the answer.

1. The bug could do _____.

      no tricks   many tricks   one trick

Make a box under the answer.

2. The bug was very _____.   sick   small   big

Make a box over the answer.

3. Who grabbed the bug? the girl inside the _____

      tent   house   horse

Fill in the blank.

4. Now the bug is the _____ of a show.

Every glip is red.   Tom is a glip.

What do you know about Tom? _____

Make a line under the answers.

1. Who tossed the phone book out of the window?
       a boy   Ott   Kim

2. Who picked up the phone book?
       a boy   Ott   Kim

Fill in the blanks.

3. Who found the phone number for a van? _____

4. Who said, "Can I go with you?" _____

Make a box around the answers.

5. Did the boy lead Kim to Jane Street or Jan Street?
       Jan Street   Jane Street

6. Could that boy read very well?
       Yes   No

7. What did Kim give the boy?
       a vane   dental care   a van

Jill made all the dresses with buttons.

Circle every dress that Jill made.

Fill in the blanks.

1. Carla told the old genie to hold a _____ on her head.

2. Did the old genie get wet? _____

3. Did Carla take her genie vow? _____

The con fox said, "I want some honey. But every time I take some honey from the bees, the bees chase me away. I need to trick the bees."

The con fox called, "Oh, bees. There are flowers by the stream. Why don't you go to those flowers?"

The bees said, "That silly fox thinks he can fool us. He wants our honey." The bees chased the fox away.

Circle the answer.

1. The con fox wanted _____.   bees   birds   honey

Make a box around the answer.

2. The fox tried to _____ the bees.   trick   eat   find

Fill in the blanks.

3. He told them about some flowers near the _____.

4. Did the trick work? _____

Every tiger is mean.   Zag is a tiger.

What do you know about Zag? _____

Side 2

Name _____

A.

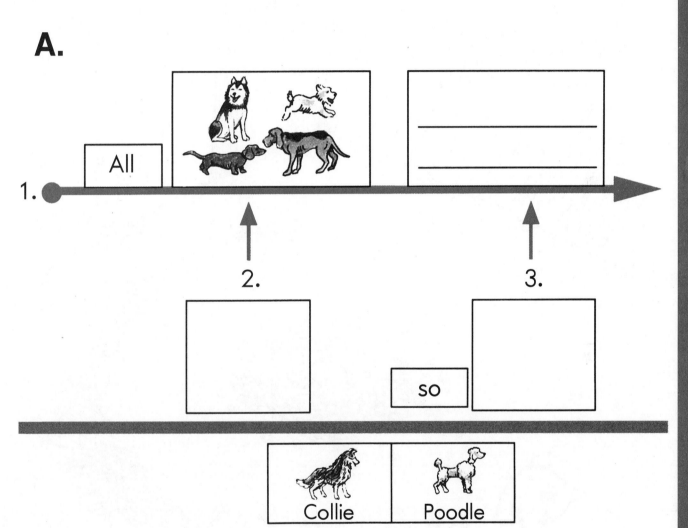

B.

Name _____

Name _____

Fill in the blank.

1. What is the title of this story?

_____

Circle the answers.

2. What did Ellen's brother need?

      water   food   a bed

3. What was in the bottom of the hole?

      water   food   Ellen's brother

Fill in the blanks.

4. Was the hole very wide? _____

5. Ellen and her brother dropped stones into the _____.

6. Did the stones make the water go up or down? _____

7. Did Ellen and her brother drink water? _____

All of the white horses can run fast.

Circle every horse that can run fast.

Side 1

Fill in the blanks.

1. How many mean ghosts lived with Boo? _____

2. The monster had made the king into a _____ .

3. The monster had a gold _____ .

Once there was a chicken that wanted to be a fox. It would chase all the other chickens, jump at them, and yell at them. All the other chickens would run away saying, "That chicken is a nut."

One day a real fox came along. The real fox saw the chicken and said, "What are you?"

The chicken said, "I am a fox."

The fox said, "I think I will eat this fox." The fox began to chase the chicken.

The chicken said, "I am tired of being a fox. I will be a chicken now." And the chicken flew away.

Make a box around the answers.

1. What did the chicken want to be?   a fox   a box   a man

2. Who did the chicken meet?   a boy   a fox   a box

Fill in the blanks.

3. Who said, "I think I'll eat this fox"? _____

4. Who said, "I am tired of being a fox"? _____

Every boy has long pants.   Bob is a boy.

What does Bob have? _____

Side 2

Make a line under the answers.

1. Carl was a _____ .

    ran   mouse   cat

2. The other mice wanted something to _____ .

    drink   look at   eat

Circle the answer.

3. Who went out to find food for the other mice?

    Carl   Fred   a crow

Fill in the blanks.

4. Who did Carl see? _____

5. What did the crow have in his mouth?

_____

6. Did Carl get the cheese? _____

Every man with a hat will go fishing.

Circle every man who will go fishing.

Fill in the blanks.

1. The old genie told the
   teacher that a girl had found a _____.

2. Did the teacher think that Ott should go to the bottle? _____

3. What did Ott make when he
   tried to make a loud sound? _____

Chickens are not the only animals that lay
eggs. A chicken is a bird, and all birds lay eggs.
So do snakes and alligators. Turtles and fish also
lay eggs. Did you know that ants and other
bugs lay eggs? The egg holds the baby animal.
A baby turtle comes out of an egg. And a baby
snake comes out of an egg. Baby chickens come
from the kind of eggs that you eat.

Make a box under the answer.

1. Are chickens the only animals that lay eggs?   Yes   No

Make a line over the answer.

2. All _____ lay eggs.   rabbits   birds   monkeys

Fill in the blank.

3. What does an egg hold? a baby _____

Circle the answer.

4. What is the best title for this story?

        Chickens Lay Eggs   Animals That Lay Eggs   The Baby Snake

Every crow likes bugs.   Jane is a crow.

What does Jane like? _____

Side 2

Name _____

Fill in the blanks.

1. What is the title of this story?

_____

2. Who grabbed a fly and ate it? _____

Make a box around the answer.

3. Who jumped way up?

        a turtle   a snake   a frog

Fill in the blanks.

4. Did the turtle jump way up? _____

5. Was the frog nice to the turtle? _____

Circle the answer.

6. Did the turtle feel happy or sad?

        happy   sad

Every big box has kittens in it.

Circle every box with kittens in it.

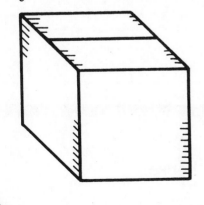

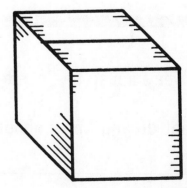

Fill in the blanks.

1. Who planted seeds in the slop? _____

2. Who told Sid, "I will teach you to read"? _____

3. Did the boss teach Sid to read well? _____

A weed is a plant that people don't want. In
some parts of the world, a rose is called a
weed. We think a rose is a pretty flower. But it
is a weed when it grows where nobody wants it.
And we like some plants that grow like weeds in
other parts of the world.

Fill in the blanks.

1. A weed is a _____ that people don't _____.

2. Could a pretty flower be a weed? _____

3. Could a big plant be a weed? _____

4. A plant that you buy is not a _____.

5. Could a rose be a weed? _____

Every house has windows.   I made a house.

What do you know about the house I made?

_____

Name _____

Circle the answers.

1. What was Flame?

    a woman   a snake   a frog

2. Could the turtle do things the frog could do?

    Yes   No

Fill in the blanks.

3. What is the title of this story?

    _____

4. Who told the turtle that
   he looked like a toenail? _____

Make a line under the answer.

5. Who was looking for frogs?

    a turtle   a snake   a frog

Fill in the blank.

6. Did the turtle tell a lie to the snake? _____

Jane will buy every bottle that is little and round.

Circle every bottle that Jane will buy.

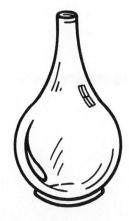    

Side 1

Fill in the blanks.

1. Did Ott give the mean boys
   a spanking or a banking? _____

2. What did Ott make when
   he tried to make a hot dog? _____

3. Where did Ott send Carla
   when he tried to send her home? _____

Some caves are holes under the ground.
Some caves are small and some are big. Small
animals like to sleep in caves that are on the
sides of mountains. Some caves are very big. In
one big cave you could walk for over 80 miles.
You could walk for days and days and not see
every part of the cave. And you would never
see the sun while you were in that cave. The
cave is under the ground, and things are
very dark there.

Fill in the blanks.

1. Some caves are big _____ under the _____.

2. Are all caves big? _____

3. If you were in a big cave, would you see the sun? _____

4. In one big cave you could walk for over _____ miles.

5. In that cave, you could walk for _____ and _____.

Every bottle is made of glass.   I have a bottle.

What do you know about the bottle I have?

_____

Worksheet 70   Name _____

| Circle the answer. |

1. Did the turtle lie to the snake?   Yes   No

| Fill in the blanks. |

2. What's the title of this story? _____

_____

3. Was Flame fast? _____

4. Was Flame a sneak? _____

| Make a box around the answers. |

5. Where did the frog jump when Flame was chasing him?

   into the weeds   into the pond   into a tree

6. Who said, "I'll bite you on the nose"?

   the frog   the snake   the turtle

| Fill in the blank. |

7. Did the snake try to bite the turtle? _____

Every dog with long ears is named Sandy.

Circle every dog named Sandy.

Side 1

Fill in the blanks.

1. Kim could not _____ well.

2. What did Kim get when she tried to phone for a van? _____

3. What did Kim get when she tried to phone for a truck? _____

Trees have roots. The roots are under the ground. The roots hold the tree up and keep it from falling over. The roots also carry water from the ground to the tree. So the roots do two things. They hold the tree up and they bring water to the tree. Trees could not live if they did not have roots.

Fill in the blanks.

1. All trees have _____.

2. Where are the roots? under the _____

3. How many things do the roots do?_____

4. They keep the tree from _____ over.

5. They bring _____ to the tree.

6. Could trees live if they didn't have roots? _____

Every girl has a short dress.   Terry is a girl.

What do you know about her? _____

Name _____

A.

| The porcupine goes 5 feet each second. |
| The mouse goes 4 feet each second. |

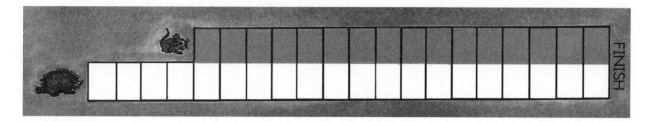

a. ____ b. ____ c. ____ d. at the ____ e. ____

B.

Name _____

Fill in the blanks.

1. What is the title of this story? _____

_____

2. Did Flame try to bite the turtle? _____

Make a line under the answers.

3. Flame hit her tooth on the turtle's _____ .

      nose   shell   ear

4. Flame said, "I think I broke my _____ ."

      nose   shell   tooth

Fill in the blanks.

5. Did the turtle let Flame go after the frog? _____

6. Was the turtle happy? _____

Ann has all the dogs with spots.

Circle every dog that Ann has.

Side 1

Fill in the blanks.

1. Did Kim think she called for
   a rental car or for dental care? _____

2. Who helped Kim call for a van? _____

3. What did Kim give the boy for helping her? _____

Some caves are big holes under the ground.
Animals live in some of the big caves. These
animals are fish and bugs. They spend all their
time in the dark. They never see the sun. And
they are very strange. Most of them are white.
They cannot see because they never have to use
their eyes. Remember the two ways that they are
strange: they cannot see, and they are white.

Fill in the blanks.

1. The animals that live in big caves are _____ and _____ .

2. What color are most of these animals? _____

3. Can these animals see? _____

4. These animals never see the _____ .

5. Is it light or dark in the big caves? _____

6. So do these animals need eyes that see? _____

| All kites are red. | Mom has a kite. |

What do you know about her kite? _____

Side 2

Make a line over the answers.

1. Who slid into the weeds?

      the turtle   the snake   the frog

2. Who bit the snake?

      the turtle   the snake   the frog

Fill in the blanks.

3. Where did the frog hide? _____

4. Could he jump well in the weeds? _____

Circle the answers.

5. Did the frog come out of the weeds?   Yes   No

6. Does Flame go after the frog any more?   Yes   No

Ted made every coat that is white.

Circle every coat that Ted made.

Side 1

Fill in the blanks.

1. Did Ellen and her brother take a train or fly? _____

2. What did Ellen's brother need? _____

3. What did the eagles drop into the hole? _____

Once there was a frog that liked to stick to things. One day, the frog said, "I will stick to this log." But the frog did not stick to a log. The frog stuck to an alligator's nose.

The alligator said, "I will open my mouth and the frog will fall in." The alligator opened her mouth. The frog did not fall in. The frog just stuck to the alligator's nose.

The frog said, "I like this log. It goes up and down. I will stick here all day." And he did.

Fill in the blanks.

1. Who liked to stick to things? _____

2. Did the frog stick to a log? _____

3. He stuck to an alligator's _____ .

Circle the answers.

4. Who opened her mouth?   a frog   an alligator   a log

5. Did the frog like to stick on the alligator's nose?   Yes   No

Fill in the blanks.

6. The alligator's nose went _____ and _____ .

All rabbits hop.   Al has a rabbit.

What does Al's rabbit do? _____

Side 2

Make a box around the answer.

1. The boy watched _____.

      mountain lions   wolves   sheep

Fill in the blanks.

2. What's the title of this story?

_____

3. Was the boy a hard worker? _____

Circle the answer.

4. Who yelled "Wolf" when there was no wolf?

      the lion   the boy   the sheep

Fill in the blanks.

5. Did a real wolf come after the sheep? _____

6. Did the people in the town believe the boy? _____

7. Was the boy good at his job after that? _____

Every bug with a tail is a zerm.

Circle every zerm.

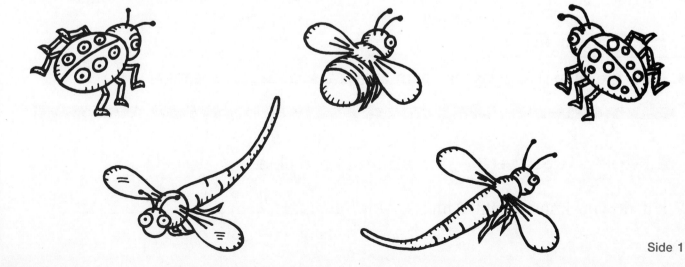

Side 1

Fill in the blanks.

1. The other mice sent Carl out for _____ .

2. Who did Carl see in a tree? _____

3. What did that crow have in his mouth? _____

Pat was a bug that could fly. But Pat did not fly. She swam. The other bugs said, "You should not be swimming. You should be flying."

Just then a flock of birds came over head. One of the bugs said, "We cannot stay here. The birds will get us. We will fly."

Pat said, "If you fly, a bird will eat you. Follow me." And she dove into the water. So all the bugs swam away. They were safe from the birds.

Now the bugs say, "Pat is right. It is fun to swim."

Circle the answer.

1. Pat liked to _____ .   fly   talk   swim

Fill in the blank.

2. Who said, "You should be flying"? _____

Make a line under the answer.

3. A flock of _____ came over.   birds   sheep   bugs

Fill in the blank.

4. Did the bugs fly away or swim away? _____ away

All cookies are sweet.   Ann has a cookie.

What do you know about Ann's cookie? _____

Make a line over the answers.

1. Who said, "I am so fast that nobody can beat me in a race"?

     the rabbit   the owl   the turtle

2. Who said, "I will race with you"?

     the rabbit   the owl   the turtle

Fill in the blanks.

3. Did the rabbit say she would stop saying
   how fast she was if she didn't win the race? _____

4. Did the rabbit and the turtle plan to
   have a long race or a short race? _____

5. Who said "Go" at the start of the race? _____

6. Who went down the path like a
   shot, the rabbit or the turtle? _____

Roy will smell every little flower.

Circle every flower that Roy will smell.

Side 1

Fill in the blanks.

1. Where did Kim want to move? to the other _____

2. Did Kim want a van or a vane? _____

3. Did Kim want a truck or a trunk? _____

4. Did Kim want dental care or a rental car? _____

There was a fox who liked to steal food. He would wait for one of the other animals to get some food. Then the fox would scare the animal away and eat the food. All the animals were mad at him.

One day a mouse said, "I will stop that fox from stealing." The mouse hid a hot pepper in some food.

The fox scared the mouse away from the food. Then the fox ate the food. The fox jumped around and ran around and yelled, "My mouth is on fire." Now the fox does not steal food from the other animals.

Fill in the blank.

1. Who liked to steal food? _____

Make a line over the answer.

2. Who stopped him from stealing?

     the fox   the mouse   the alligator

Circle the answer.

3. What did the mouse leave for the fox?

     a pepper   an apple   an alligator

All pips are good to eat.   Jane ate a pip.

What do you know about the pip Jane ate?

_____

Name _____

Make a box around the answers.

1. The other animals wanted the _____ to win the race.

owl   turtle   rabbit

2. But the _____ went down the path like a shot.

owl   turtle   rabbit

Fill in the blanks.

3. Who stopped to rest under a big tree? _____

4. Did the rabbit go to sleep? _____

5. Who said, "I'll just keep going"? _____

Circle the answers.

6. Who said, "Come on, turtle"?

the rabbit   the turtle   the other animals

7. Did the rabbit win the race?   Yes   No

Linda made all of the big cakes.

Circle all the cakes Linda made.

Fill in the blanks.

1. Flame hit her tooth on the turtle's _____

2. Did the turtle let Flame go after the frog? _____

3. Could the frog jump well in the weeds? _____

The tall man always went to sleep in the bed. But he made his dog sleep on the floor. The dog said, "I must use my head, head, head and find a way to get in bed, bed, bed."

So the dog jumped up and yelled. "I hear a wolf in the yard." The tall man ran after the wolf. The dog locked the door and said, "Now that I locked the door, door, door, I won't sleep on the floor, floor, floor."

Make a circle over the answer.

1. The tall man made the dog sleep on _____.

    the floor   the bed   the mat

Make a box under the answer.

2. The tall man went to sleep _____.

    on the floor   in the bed   on a mat

Fill in the blanks.

3. Who said, "I hear a wolf in the yard"? _____

4. Who went after the wolf? _____

All rats have teeth.   Dan has two rats.

What do you know about Dan's rats? _____

Side 2

A.

Name _____

striped	bike	rode	patch	pants	small	shirt	wore

B.

washed	mopped	read	painted	book
window	floor	piano		

C.

Name _____

1. My brother and my sister had pet pigs. <u>They</u> just loved to roll around in the mud.

2. We always kept a glass on top of the refrigerator. We kept <u>it</u> full of water.

Side 2

Name _____

Fill in the blank.

1. What is the title of this story?

_____

Make a line over the answers.

2. Who said, "I want to be your friend"?

   the rabbit   the lion   the mouse

3. Who said, "I am the king of all the animals"?

   the rabbit   the lion   the mouse

Fill in the blanks.

4. What did the lion get in his paw? _____

5. Could the elephant get the thorn? _____

6. Could the alligator get the thorn? _____

7. Who got the thorn? _____

8. Are the lion and the mouse good friends now? _____

Every big fish likes bugs.

Circle every fish that likes bugs.

Fill in the blanks.

1. How many mean ghosts lived with Boo? _____

2. Which ghost could read the words on the gold rod? _____

3. Are the people in Boo's town afraid of ghosts now? _____

The tall man went riding on his bike. His dog ran next to him. The dog said, "I would like, like, like to ride that bike, bike, bike." But the tall man would not let the dog ride his bike.
Soon the man stopped to talk to his friends. The dog jumped on the bike and started to ride. He saw a tree. He tried to ride around it, but the bike hit the tree. The dog fell to the ground. The dog said, "I do not like, like, like to ride a bike, bike, bike."

Fill in the blanks.

1. The tall _____ went riding on his _____ .

Make a box over the answer.

2. Did the tall man let the dog ride the bike?   Yes   No

Fill in the blanks.

3. Why did the man stop riding? _____

4. Who jumped on the bike? _____

5. What did the dog hit? a _____

All dogs have bones.   Spot is a dog.

So what does Spot have? _____

Side 2

Name _____

Make a box around the answers.

1. What was Casey?

       a lion   a fox   a mouse   a rabbit

2. Which animal liked to steal hens from a barn?

       a lion   a fox   a mouse   a rabbit

Fill in the blanks.

3. What is the title of this story? _____

4. Who would chase the fox into the lake? _____

Make a line over the answers.

5. What did the fox put out for Casey to eat?

       a salad   a hen   a rabbit

6. Casey said, "Don't throw me into the _____."

       thorn trees   thorn bushes   lake

7. Casey said, "I'm Casey the rabbit, and you can't _____ me."

       thorn   hurt   hunt   kiss

If a boy is tall and smiling, he has a brother.

Circle every boy who has a brother.

Side 1

Fill in the blanks.

1. Who said, "I am so fast that
   nobody can beat me in a race"? _____

2. Who said, "I will race with you"? _____

3. Could the turtle run as fast as the rabbit? _____

An ant is an insect. A fly is an insect. A butterfly is an insect. A grasshopper is an insect. Is a spider an insect? No. A spider looks like other insects, but it is not an insect. The body of any insect has three parts. The body of an ant has three parts. The body of a butterfly has three parts. But the body of a spider does not have three parts. So a spider is not an insect.

Fill in the blanks.

1. Name three insects. _____ _____ _____

2. How many parts does the body of an insect have? _____

3. How many parts does the body of an ant have? _____

4. Is a spider an insect? _____

5. Why isn't a spider an insect?_____

_____

Every table has legs.   I have a table.

What do you know about my table? _____

Side 2

Fill in the blanks.

1. What is the title of this story? _____

2. What was Mr. Hall afraid of? _____

3. Was he more afraid of big dogs or little dogs? _____

Circle the answers.

4. Mr. Hall went on a _____.   hill   dog   ship

5. Where was he going?

        to Japan   to the U.S.   to Rome

Make a line over the answer.

6. What did he see on the deck of the ship?

        a snake   a dog   a bike

Fill in the blanks.

7. Did the ship sink? _____

8. Did Mr. Hall find a raft or a life boat? _____

9. Who swam closer and closer to him? _____

There is a dog behind every box that has toys in it.

Circle every box that has a dog behind it.

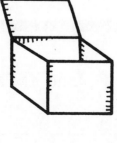

Fill in the blanks.

1. Ott went to a school for _____.

2. Carla found a yellow _____.

3. How many teachers are now teaching in the genie school? _____

4. What are their names? _____

People once believed the world was flat. They said, "If you sail to the end of the sea, you will fall off."

One man said, "I think the world is round. I think I could sail all the way around the world without falling off." The man got a big ship and many men. He went on a long trip in that ship. He found a new land that people didn't know about. The name of that place is America.

Fill in the blanks.

1. Long ago, people used to think the world was _____.

2. One man said, "I think the world is _____."

3. Is the world round or flat? _____

Every rimp is an animal.   Jane has a rimp.

What do you know about her rimp? _____

Name _____

| Make a box around the answers. |

1. After the ship went down, Mr. Hall found a _____.

    boat   bike   raft

2. What swam to his raft?   a dog   a goat   a man

| Circle the answers. |

3. Did Mr. Hall sit near the dog?   Yes   No

4. What did Mr. Hall toss to the dog?

    meat   crackers   dog food   a snake

5. What came near the raft?

    a bike   a raft   a man   a ship

| Fill in the blanks. |

6. Could the people hear Mr. Hall? _____

7. Who could they hear? _____

8. Does Mr. Hall like the dog now? _____

If a lady has long hair and a long dress, she is a mother.

Circle every mother.

Fill in the blanks.

1. Did the other animals want the
   rabbit or the turtle to win the race? _____

2. Who fell asleep under the big tree? _____

3. Did the turtle win the race? _____

There was a girl who sucked her thumb. She
made loud sounds when she sucked her thumb. Her
mom and dad got mad at her, but she did not stop
sucking her thumb.
   Then one day the dog saw her sucking her thumb.
The dog said, "That thumb looks good." So when
the girl put her thumb down, the dog began to lick
it. Now the girl does not suck her thumb any more.

Make a circle under the answer.

1. A girl _____ her thumb.

   socked   sucked   painted

Make a circle over the answer.

2. Her mom and _____ got mad at her.

   dog   brother   dad

Fill in the blanks.

3. Who said, "That thumb looks good"? _____

4. Now the _____ does not _____

   her _____ .

All bump weeds are sweet.   Carol has a bump weed.

What do you know about her bump weed? _____

Name _____

| Circle the answer. |

1. The title of this story is The Prince _____ .

     and the Girl   and the Ramp   and the Tramp

| Fill in the blanks. |

2. Who said, "Everybody loves me"? _____

3. Did the prince meet a ramp or a tramp? _____

| Make a box around the answer. |

4. Who put on the prince's robe?

     the tramp   the people   the king

| Fill in the blanks. |

5. The prince dressed like the _____ .

6. Were the people nice to the real prince? _____

7. Who did the tramp live with
   at the end of the story? _____

If it is fat and has 4 legs, it is a ronk.

Circle every ronk.

Fill in the blanks.

1. Who was the king of the other animals? _____

2. Who said, "I want to be your friend"? _____

3. What did the mouse pull from the lion's paw? _____

     Do you remember about insects? An ant is an insect. A grasshopper is an insect. A fly is an insect. All insects have a body with three parts. A spider is not an insect because a spider does not have a body with three parts. A spider's body has two parts. Here is something else about insects. All insects have six legs. Spiders do not have six legs. Spiders have 8 legs.

Fill in the blanks.

1. All insects have _____ legs.

2. Name three animals that have six legs. _____

   _____   _____

3. How many legs do spiders have? _____

4. How many parts does a spider's body have? _____

5. How many parts does an insect's body have? _____

All cakes are food.   I made a cake.

What do you know about my cake? _____

Side 2

Name _____

A.

| wore | collar | spots | chewed | bone |

B.

| she | stood | wore | brush | chair | hat | used |

Name _____

C. 1. My brother and my sister had pet pigs.

<u>They</u> just loved to roll around in the mud.

2. We always kept a glass on top of the refrigerator.

We kept <u>it</u> full of water.

Side 2

Fill in the blanks.

1. What is the title of this story? _____

_____

2. Who said, "Sleep hard"? _____

Circle the answers.

3. Did Jean sleep hard?   Yes   No

4. Who did Jean meet?   a dog   a wizard   a lady

Fill in the blanks.

5. The wizard told her, "All _____ are mean."

6. Did Jean see strange animals? _____

Make a line over the answer.

7. The name of the land in Jean's dream was the land of _____.

peevish pets   many pits   peevish pits

Circle the right rule.

8. All crumps are mean.   All little drumps are mean.

Some little crumps are mean. All little crumps are mean.

Every boy with a coat and a hat is hungry.

Circle every boy who is hungry.

Fill in the blanks.

1. Who said, "Don't throw me in the thorn bushes"? _____

2. Did the thorn bushes hurt Casey? _____

3. Casey said, "I'm Casey the rabbit and you can't _____ me."

If you jumped from a ladder, you would go down. If you jumped from a plane, you would fall down. But if you were very, very far from the ground, things would not be the same. When you are very, very far from the ground, you are in space. Things don't fall in space. If you stepped from a ladder in space, you would float. You would not go down. Things do not fall in space. So there is no up or down in space.

Fill in the blanks.

1. When you are very, very far from the ground, you are in _____.

2. Do things fall when you are near the ground? _____

3. Do things fall when you are in space? _____

4. If you stepped from a ladder in space, you would _____.

5. There is no _____ or _____ in space.

All mips are green.   Mom has a mip.

What do you know about her mip? _____

Side 2

Name _____

Fill in the blanks.

1. What was the name of the
   land Jean was in? the land of _____

2. What kind of crumps are mean? _____

3. Who told Jean how to
   make the mean crumps go away? _____

4. How many rules did Jean have to know before she could go home? _____

Make a line over the answers.

5. What did Jean say to make the crumps go away?

   "Away."   "Go away, away."   "Away, away."   "Get out of here."

6. Did the mean crump go away when Jean said that?

   Yes   No

Fill in the blank.

7. What is the title of this story?

   _____

If it has spots and two ears, it is a glim.

Circle every glim.

Fill in the blanks.

1. What was Mr. Hall afraid of? _____

2. Did the ship sink? _____

3. Who got on the raft with Mr. Hall? _____

Once there was a hound that was very tired. The hound did not have a place to sleep. And the night was cold and wet. So the hound began to howl. "Owww," he said.

He woke the people up. They got mad. They tossed socks, hats, shoes, and coats at the hound. They tossed things until there was a big pile of stuff.

Then the dog said, "Now I have a place to sleep." So the dog went to sleep in the pile of socks, hats, shoes, and coats.

Make a box around the answer.

1. The hound was very _____ .

   happy   fast   old   tired

Make a line under the answer.

2. But he did not have a place to _____ .

   eat   hide   sleep

Fill in the blanks.

3. So he began to _____ .

4. Then the dog said, "Now I have a _____ to _____ ."

All mip food is in a can.   Dan has mip food.

What do you know about Dan's mip food? _____

Side 2

Fill in the blanks.

1. All _____ crumps are _____ .

2. Jean was in the land of _____ _____ .

3. How many rules did Jean have
   to know before she could go home? _____

4. What did she say to make mean crumps go away? _____

5. Every dusty path leads _____ .

Circle the answers.

6. Who told Jean the rule about the dusty paths?
   　　　 a wizard 　　　 a crump 　　　 her mother

7. The water in the lake was _____ .
   　　　 pink 　　　 red 　　　 deep

Fill in the blanks.

8. Could Jean get away from the lake by taking a dusty path? _____

9. Why not? _____

_____

Find out where the bugs are.

Here is the rule: Every white house has bugs.

　　　 Kim's house is brown.
　　　 Spot's house is white.
　　　 Ott's house is white.
　　　 Tim's house is red.
　　　 Mom's house is black.

Who has a house with bugs? _____

All feps are words.   Carmen has feps.

What do you know about Carmen's feps? _____

There was a bug who couldn't run. "I will teach you to run," a wolf said. "Move your legs very fast."

The bug tried it. "No," the wolf said. "You are dancing, not running. Move up and down."

The bug tried. "No," the wolf said. "You are hopping."

The wolf showed her teeth. The bug got scared and ran faster than any bug you have ever seen.

| Fill in the blanks. |
1. The _____ said, "I will teach you to _____."

| Make a circle over the answer. |
2. First the wolf told the bug to move his legs _____.

    up and down   here and there   very fast

| Make a box under the answer. |
3. Then the wolf told the bug to move _____.

    up and down   here and there   very fast

| Fill in the blanks. |
4. The _____ got scared and _____

faster than any _____ you have ever seen.

Name _____

Make a line under the answers.

1. The dusty paths led right back _____ .

    to the mountain   to the lake   to a cake

2. Before Jean could leave the land of peevish pets, she had to know _____ .

    sixteen rules   one more rule   twenty rules

Fill in the blanks.

3. The wizard told her that
   every rocky path leads _____ .

4. What did Jean see all around the mountain? _____

5. Who ran after Jean? _____

6. What did Jean say to make
   the mean crumps go away? _____

Find out who will go to Japan.

Here is the rule: The people who are running will go to Japan.

    The boss is running.
    Ellen is running.
    Boo is sitting.
    Jean is standing.
    The turtle is not running.

Who will go to Japan? _____ _____

All glicks are small.   Ann has a glick.

What do you know about her glick? _____

━━

There was a dog that said, "I hate to take a bath."
That dog had bugs. The dog said, "I hate bugs."
One day a man said, "That dog has bugs, so I will give
the dog a bath."
The dog said, "I hate baths."
His bugs said, "We hate baths, too."
The man gave the dog a bath, and the bugs went away.
Now the dog says, "I like baths. They made my bugs go away."

| Fill in the blanks. |

1. Did the dog like baths or hate baths? _____ baths

2. Who said, "We hate baths, too"? _____

3. Who said, "I will give the dog a bath"? _____

4. Why does the dog like baths now?

_____

Fill in the blanks.

1. What is the title of this story?

_____

2. Who told the rule about red food? _____

3. What is the rule about red food?

_____

Make a line under the answers.

4. Did Jean eat the ice cream?   Yes   No

5. Did Jean eat the red banana?   Yes   No

6. Did Jean eat the white grapes?   Yes   No

Find out who has frogs.

Rule: There are frogs in every tin cup.

Ellen has a tin cup.
Ott does not have a tin cup.
Sid has a tin cup.
Spot does not have a tin cup.
Boo has a tin cup.

Who has frogs? _____ _____ _____

Side 1

All flying bats are mammals.   Fred is a flying bat.

What do you know about him? _____

Some trees have very good wood. Other trees have wood that is not so good. The good wood is made into tables and chairs and other wooden things. Do you know what happens to the wood that is not so good? It is made into paper. The next time you use some paper, remember that you are using a tree.

Fill in the blank.

1. Do all trees have very good wood? _____

Circle the answers.

2. Good wood is made into _____.

  windows and streets   tables and chairs   paper

3. Wood that is not so good is made into _____.

  paper   tables and chairs   streets

Make a line under the answer.

4. What is the best title for this story?

  Some Trees Have Good Wood

  Tables and Chairs Are Made of Wood

  Paper Comes from Trees

Name _____

A.

1. ● All ——————————————————————→

2. ↑   3. ↑

   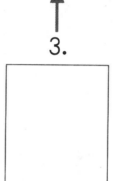

[ ]   [ ]

a. good   bad
b. good   bad
c. good   bad

B.

| legs | wheels | smiled | held | screwdriver |

Name _____

C. Mother held Baby Sarah as she drank from a baby bottle.

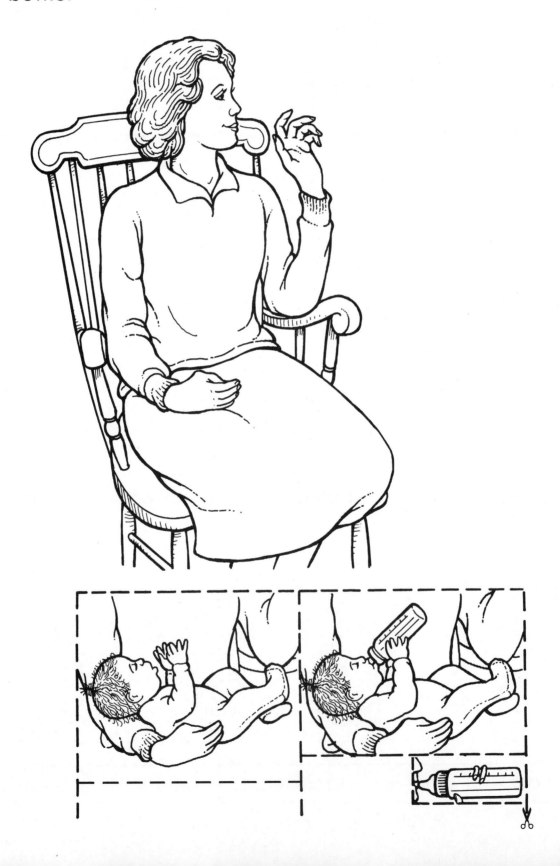

Side 2

Name _____

Fill in the blanks.

1. What is the name of the
   land in Jean's dream? _____

2. How many rules did she have
   to know before she could leave? _____

3. What did Jean know
   about all little crumps? _____

4. What do you do to make
   a mean crump go away? _____

5. What kind of path goes to the lake? _____

6. What kind of path
   goes to the mountain? _____

7. What kind of food is good to eat? _____

8. What happened to Jean when she ate three red bananas?

   _____

9. Was Jean happy or sad? _____

Find out which girls are sitting on a pin.

Rule: Every girl who is crying is sitting on a pin.

       Ned is laughing.
       Peg is not crying.
       Pam is crying.
       Jane is playing ball.
       Linda is crying.

Which girls are sitting on a pin? _____ _____

Every lion is sleepy.   Peg is a lion.

What do you know about her? _____

Did you know that glass melts? If a bottle gets very hot, it can melt. First, the bottle will become soft. When the bottle gets hotter and hotter, the glass will start to turn red. When the glass is very, very hot, it will flow like water. Watch out when glass melts. It is very, very hot.

| Circle the answer. |

1. The best title for this story is _____ .

   Glass Melts   Glass Becomes Soft   A Bottle

| Fill in the blanks. |

2. If a bottle gets very hot, what happens first?

   It will become _____ .

3. What color will the bottle become? _____

4. Then the glass will flow like _____ .

5. Should you touch glass when it is melting? _____

| Make a line under the answer. |

6. Does glass melt?   Yes   No

Name _____

Fill in the blanks.

1. What's the title of this story? _____

   _____

2. What happened to Jean when she ate three red bananas? _____

   _____

3. Who told Jean how to make the stripes disappear? _____

4. "If you _____ in the lake, the stripes _____

   _____ ."

5. Which path did Jean take to the lake? _____

Find out who is going to the store.

Rule: If a boy is in the park, he is going to the store.

   Jack is in the school.
   Bob is in the park.
   Pam is in the house.
   Tom is in the park.
   Ted is in the bedroom.

Who is going to the store? _____ _____

Every cup has a handle.   I have a cup.

What do you know about the cup I have? _____

     A man named Isaac Newton lived a long time back. One day he was sitting under a tree. An apple dropped on his head. He began to think about that apple. He made up a rule about things. Here is his rule: "What goes up must come down."

Fill in the blanks.

1. Who was sitting under the tree? _____

2. What dropped on his head? _____

3. Newton made up a _____ .

4. "What goes _____ must come _____."

Name _____

| Fill in the blanks. |

1. Why did Jean have red stripes? _____

   _____

2. What did she have to do to make the stripes disappear?

   _____

| Circle the answers. |

3. Which path did she take to the lake?

   the muddy path   the dusty path   the rocky path

4. How many little crumps were on the path?

   five   six   one   three

5. What did she say to make the crumps go away?

   "Away, you crumps."   "Away."   "Away, away."

| Fill in the blanks. |

6. Did the stripes disappear when she jumped into the lake? _____

7. What color was her hair now? _____

8. If you stand _____, the white hair will go away.

Find out who ate crackers.

Rule: The people who ate crackers are sleeping.

   Jane is playing ball.
   Jean is sleeping.
   Tim is sleeping.
   The boss is yelling at Sid.
   Ellen is sleeping.

Who ate crackers? _____ _____ _____

Side 1

All weeds are plants.   Marta has a weed.

What do you know about Marta's weed? _____

Here is a rule about all living things: All living things grow, and all living things need water. Is a tree a living thing? Yes. So you know that a tree grows, and you know that a tree needs water. A dog is a living thing. So what do you know about a dog? You know a dog grows. You know that a dog needs water. You are a living thing. Do you grow? Yes. Do you need water? Yes.

Fill in the blanks.

1. All living things _____.

2. All living things need _____.

3. Is a fly a living thing? _____

4. Name two things you know about a fly. _____

   _____

5. Is a dog a living thing? _____

6. So you know that a dog _____.

   And you know that a dog needs _____.

7. Is a chair a living thing? _____

8. Does a chair need water? _____

Side 2

Fill in the blanks.

1. What did Jean do to make the stripes disappear?

   _____

2. What color was her hair after she jumped in the lake? _____

3. What's the title of this story?_____

   _____

4. What did Jean do to make
   the white disappear? _____

Make a line under the answers.

5. Now Jean was _____ .

      big   bald   green   old

6. What did Jean have to do to get her hair back?

      clamp her hands   clap her hands   clamp her teeth

Find out who has cash.

Rule: Every red bottle has cash in it.

      Sandy has a red bottle.
      Tom has four yellow bottles.
      The boss has two red bottles.
      Mom has one red bottle.
      Spot has a red dish.

Who has cash? _____ _____ _____

All rits are little.   Sop is a rit.

What do you know about Sop? _____

Remember the rule about living things: All living things grow, and all living things need water. Here is another rule about all living things. All living things make babies. A tree is a living thing. A tree makes baby trees. A fish is a living thing. A fish makes baby fish. A spider is a living thing. A spider makes baby spiders. Remember the rule: All living things make babies.

Fill in all the blanks.

1. What do all living things make? _____

2. Is a fish a living thing? _____

3. So a fish makes _____ _____ .

4. Is a spider a living thing? _____

5. So a spider makes _____ _____ .

6. Is a chair a living thing? _____

7. Does a chair make baby chairs? _____

8. Name two things you know about living things.

   All living things _____ .

   All living things need _____ .

Make a box around the answers.

1. Did Jean get her hair back?   Yes   No

2. What color was her hair?

           red   yellow   white

Make a line under the answer.

3. A _____ animal came out of the lake.

           sitting   talking   smiling

Fill in the blanks.

4. Did the animal tell Jean the right rule about dusty paths? _____

5. Did he tell Jean the right rule about jumping in the lake? _____

Circle the answer.

6. What did he tell her to say so that she could have fun?

        "Side, slide."   "Slide, slide."   "Side, side."

Find out who likes monsters.

Rule: Everybody who is smiling likes monsters.

        The boss is yelling at Jan.
        Jan is very sad.
        Ellen is smiling.
        The tiger is smiling.
        Dad has a tear in his eye.

Who likes monsters? _____ _____

All nails are made of metal.   Ann has a nail.

What do you know about her nail? _____

There once was a girl with a cold head. She said, "I need a warm hat." So she got a nice big hat. But the wind blew her hat away. The girl yelled, "My head is cold again." And she ran after her hat. She fell down in some mud. A big chunk of mud stuck to her head. The girl smiled and said, "Now my head is not cold. It is warm. This mud is better than a hat." The girl wore the mud hat for three years. Soon she had many plants growing from her hat.

| Make a box over the answer. |
1. The girl had a _____ head.

        cold   fat   big   old

| Fill in the blanks. |
2. She said, "I _____ a warm _____."

| Circle the answer. |
3. She fell in some _____.

       plants   mud   water   flowers

| Fill in the blanks. |
4. She wore the mud _____ for _____ years.

| Make a box over the answer. |
5. What is growing from the hat now?

       trees   plants   bugs

Name _____

A.

hair	glasses	smiled	long	wore

B.

The children caught butterflies. They had orange wings.

Name _____

Fill in the blanks.

1. Who told Jean what to say if
   she wanted to have fun? the _____ animal

2. He said, "If you want to have fun, say '_____.'"

3. Jean was up to her _____ in snow.

4. What do you say if you want to be cold? _____

5. What do you say if you
   want to be warm again? _____

Circle the answers.

6. Did the talking animal tell the right rule about dusty paths?

   Yes   No

7. Did he tell the right rule about having fun?

   Yes   No

8. Make up a rule about talking animals. Talking animals _____.

   do good things   lie   tell bedtime stories

Find out where the mice are.

Rule: Every big house has mice in it.

   The boss has a little house.
   Sid has a big house.
   Ann has a big horse.
   Jean has a big house.
   Sam's house is very big.

Who has a house with mice? _____ _____ _____

Side 1

All dogs sleep.   Mike is a dog.

What do you know about Mike? _____

 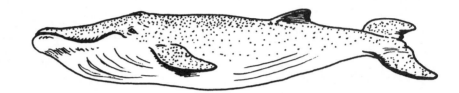

Some animals are very small. And other animals are very big. A mouse is small. A bug is even smaller. There are animals smaller than a bug. The biggest animal that lives on land is the elephant. Every day he eats a pile of grass bigger than you. But the elephant is not the biggest animal there is. The biggest animal is the whale. Whales do not live on land. Whales live in the sea. Some whales are bigger than ten elephants.

Fill in the blanks.

1. Is a mouse a big animal? _____

2. Name an animal that is smaller than a mouse. _____

3. Is a bug the smallest animal there is? _____

4. What is the biggest animal that lives on land? _____

5. Name an animal that is bigger than an elephant. _____

6. Where do whales live? _____

7. Some _____ are bigger than _____ elephants.

Side 2

Fill in the blanks.

1. What is the rule about how to be cold? _____

2. What do you say if you want to be warm again?

   _____

3. What is the rule about talking animals? Talking animals _____ .

4. If a talking animal tells you that pink ice
   cream is good, you know that pink ice cream is _____ .

Make a line over the answers.

5. Who did Jean meet? a talking _____

            bug   tree   lady

6. The bug said, "I never _____ ."

            eat   talk   sleep

Find out who has ice cream.

Rule: The animals that are taking a bath have ice cream.

       The tiger is taking a bath.
       The lion is walking with the mouse.
       The cat is taking a bath.
       The turtle is taking a bath.
       The frog is sleeping on a log.

Who has ice cream?

_____ _____ _____

All ticks have eight legs.   I have a tick.

What do you know about my tick? _____

Trees do not grow in the winter because the ground is cold. In the spring the sun begins to make the ground warmer and warmer. First the top of the ground gets warm. Then the deeper parts of the ground get warm. Every year small trees begin to grow before big trees grow. Small trees grow first because their roots are not very deep in the ground. So their roots warm up before the roots of big trees warm up.

| Fill in the blanks. |

1. When do trees begin to grow? in the _____

2. Trees do not grow in the _____ .

3. Trees begin to grow when their roots get _____ .

4. Why do small trees grow first every year? _____

_____

Name _____

Fill in the blanks.

1. What is the title of this story? _____

_____

2. What do you say if you want to be cold? _____

_____

3. What is the rule about talking animals?

_____

4. What do you say if you want to be warm again?

_____

5. Jean told the bug to tell her about something that is really _____ .

Circle the answers.

6. What happened when Jean tapped her foot three times?
   She began to _____ .

         sneak   snake   fly   cry

7. What did the strange man say to Jean?

         "Arf."   "Barn, barn."   "Bark, bark."

         "Hello, there."

Find out who is smart.

Rule: The people with hats are smart.

     Kim has a hat.
     Sid has a hat.
     The boss does not have a hat.
     Ellen has a hat.
     Spot does not have a hat.

Who is smart? _____ _____ _____   Side 1

All bikes have wheels.   Tom has a bike.

What do you know about Tom's bike? _____

     Some mountains are miles tall. The tallest mountain in the U.S. is in Alaska. It is nearly four miles tall. But it is not the tallest mountain in the world. The tallest mountain in the world is named Everest. Everest is in a land called Tibet. Everest is over five miles tall.

| Fill in the blanks. |

1. The tallest mountain in the U.S. is in _____.

2. How many miles tall is that mountain? _____

3. The tallest mountain in the world is in a land called _____.

4. That mountain is named _____.

5. Everest is over _____ miles tall.

Circle the answers.

1. Who did Jean trick? a talking _____

           cat   rat   bug   bat

2. What did Jean do so that she could fly?

         said, "side, slide"   tapped her foot three times

Fill in the blanks.

3. What is the rule about talking animals?

   _____

4. What did the man hand Jean? _____

5. If you tell the man to
   become a dog, the man becomes _____.

6. Every time Jean says, "But what and when . . . ," the wizard

   _____.

7. How many more rules did Jean
   need to leave the land of peevish pets? _____

Find out who has a bug.

Rule: Every fat bottle has a bug in it.

       Pat's bottle is fat.
       Fred's bottle is not fat.
       Don's bottle is fat.
       Ellen's bottle is not fat.
       Sandy's bottle is not fat.

Who has a bug? _____ _____

All dops are made of wood.   I have a dop.

What do you know about my dop? _____

      Do you remember which land animal is the biggest? The elephant. Which is the biggest animal of all? The whale. Where does the whale live? In the sea. But a whale is not a fish. Here is the rule: Fish breathe water. Can you breathe water? No. Can a dog breathe water? No. Can a whale breathe water? No. Whales must breathe air, just like you and me. Whales have a hole at the top of their heads. They stick their heads out of the water and breathe air. Remember, a whale is not a fish.

| Fill in the blanks. |

1. Which land animal is the biggest? _____

2. Which animal is the biggest of all? _____

3. Where does the whale live? _____

4. Can you breathe water? _____

5. Can a whale breathe water? _____

6. A whale is _____ a _____ .

Side 2

Fill in the blanks.

1. How do you make the wizard appear?

   Say, "_____."

2. How do you make the wizard disappear?

   Say, "_____."

3. What was on Jean's bed? _____

4. What was the name of the puppy? _____

5. The note said, "If you love him and _____ with him, he

   will grow up to be the _____ dog in the _____."

6. Was Jean happy or sad? _____

Find out who is a boss.

Rule: Every boss has short hair.

   Tom has short hair.
   Carol has short hair.
   Ron has long hair.
   Ellen has no hair.
   Pam has short hair.

Who is a boss? _____ _____ _____

All mups have red ears.   Ellen is a mup.

What do you know about Ellen? _____

       The first people lived thousands and thousands of years back. These people needed food, but they couldn't go to the store and buy food. There were no food stores. There were no stores of any kind. So these people had to hunt animals. But they did not have guns. They did not have arrows. So they had to use rocks and sticks to kill animals. But some animals were hard to kill. They were big and mean. The men would hide behind trees and jump out at the animal. Sometimes they would kill the animal. Sometimes the animal would get away. Sometimes the animal would kill them.

| Fill in the blanks. |

1. The first people lived _____ and

_____ of years back.

2. Could these people buy food at a store? _____

3. Did they have guns and arrows? _____

4. What did they use to kill animals? _____ and _____

5. Sometimes they would kill the animal. But sometimes

the _____ would kill them.